Behind Media

Newspapers

Catherine Chambers

Heinemann
LIBRARY

www.heinemann.co.uk/library
Visit our website to find out more information about **Heinemann Library** books.

To order:
☎ Phone 44 (0) 1865 888066
🖹 Send a fax to 44 (0) 1865 314091
💻 Visit the Heinemann Bookshop at www.heinemann.co.uk/library to browse our catalogue and order online.

First published in Great Britain by Heinemann Library, Halley Court, Jordan Hill, Oxford, OX2 8EJ,
a division of Reed Educational and Professional Publishing Ltd.
Heinemann is a registered trademark of Reed Educational and Professional Publishing Ltd.

OXFORD MELBOURNE AUCKLAND
JOHANNESBURG BLANTYRE GABORONE
IBADAN PORTSMOUTH NH (USA) CHICAGO

© Reed Educational and Professional Publishing Ltd 2001
The moral right of the proprietor has been asserted.

Designed by Paul Davies and Associates
Originated by Ambassador Litho Ltd.
Printed in Hong Kong/China

ISBN 0 431 11460 9 (hardback)   ISBN 0 431 11465 X (paperback)
06 05 04 03 02   06 05 04 03 02
10 9 8 7 6 5 4 3 2 1   10 9 8 7 6 5 4 3 2

British Library Cataloguing in Publication Data

Chambers, Catherine
  Newspapers. - (Behind Media)
  1.Newspapers - Juvenile literature
  I.Title
  070.1'72

Acknowledgements
The Publishers would like to thank the following for permission to reproduce copyright material:
Photographs: Action-Plus p25; Big Pictures p26; Trevor Clifford pp10, 14, 19, 31, 41; Corbis pp5, 40, Adrian
Arbib p15, 28, Annie Griffiths Belt p39; EPA pp18, 19; Greg Evans p13; NHPA, David Woodfall p6; PA News
p27, Barry Batchelor p43, PA News/EPA p45; Panos p29, Marcus Rose p9; Photographers' Library p20;
Popperfoto p23, Popperfoto/AFP, Pierre Verdy p35, Popperfoto/Reuters, Mitsuko Kobori-Kyodo p42, Peter
Morgan p12, Greg White p8; Science Photo Library p44; Telegraph Colour Library p24, Ron Chapple pp16,
30; Tony Stone, Roy Botterell p4, J P Williams p7; United Feature Syndicate 1993/Charles Schulz p33;
View p22.
Realia: *The Jang* (Courtesy of the Jang Group of newspapers) p10; *The Chicago Tribune* p14; *The Daily
Telegraph, Daily Mail* p19; *The Age, Diamond Valley News* (Courtesy of Leader Newspapers, Melbourne,
Australia) p31.

Cover photograph reproduced with permission of Stock Directory.

Our thanks to David English for his comments in the preparation of this book.

Every effort has been made to contact copyright holders of any material reproduced in this book.
Any omissions will be rectified in subsequent printings if notice is given to the publishers.

Picture Ladybird

Books for reading aloud with 2 – 6 year olds

The exciting *Picture Ladybird* series includes a wide range of animal stories, funny rhymes, and real life adventures that are perfect to read aloud and share at storytime or bedtime.

A whole library of beautiful books for you to collect

RHYMING STORIES

Easy to follow and great for joining in!

Jasper's Jungle Journey, Val Biro
Shoo Fly, Shoo! Brian Moses
Ten Tall Giraffes, Brian Moses
In Comes the Tide, Valerie King
Toot! Learns to Fly,
Geraldine Taylor & Jill Harker
Who Am I? Judith Nicholls
Fly Eagle, Fly! Jan Pollard

IMAGINATIVE TALES

Mysterious and magical, or just a little shivery

The Star that Fell, Karen Hayles
Wishing Moon, Lesley Harker
Don't Worry William, Christine Morton
This Way Little Badger, Phil McMylor
The Giant Walks, Judith Nicholls
Kelly and the Mermaid, Karen King

FUNNY STORIES

Make storytime good fun!

Benedict Goes to the Beach, Chris Demarest
Bella and Gertie, Geraldine Taylor
Edward Goes Exploring, David Pace
Telephone Ted, Joan Stimson
Top Shelf Ted, Joan Stimson
Helpful Henry, Shen Roddie
What's Wrong with Bertie? Tony Bradman
Bears Can't Fly, Val Biro
Finnigan's Flap, Joan Stimson

REAL LIFE ADVENTURE

Situations to explore and discover

Joe and the Farm Goose,
Geraldine Taylor & Jill Harker
Going to Playgroup,
Geraldine Taylor & Jill Harker
The Great Rabbit Race, Geraldine Taylor
Pushchair Polly, Tony Bradman

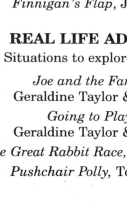

Contents

Any words appearing in the text in bold, **like this**, are explained in the Glossary.

The Importance of Print

Introduction

Nearly 400 years ago, the first printed news-sheets were distributed amongst the people of northern Germany. They included stories from far-off countries – stories that would normally have been passed on by word of mouth or perhaps written on posted notices, or maybe not spread at all. Since then, the newspaper has informed all those who are lucky enough to be able to read about their local community and the world at large. This book takes you through the processes and people involved in making the newspapers of today, from **breaking** the story to stacking the stands.

What's the big attraction?

Newspapers can be bought in many places and taken almost anywhere. They can be read in the quiet of a home or in the buzz of an office; on a plane or train or a local park bench. Unlike news broadcast on the radio or television, other people's noise will not affect the reader. We will be looking at other advantages of the newspaper, and the disadvantages, too.

*This man has chosen to read a **broadsheet** newspaper, with several sections. Different newspapers attract a particular readership, and keep it by finding out what their loyal readership wants. Newspapers in most societies give a choice of story and a choice of opinion. However, in some societies newspapers are restricted by the government in terms of content and opinion – news is often the same whichever paper the reader buys.*

Who makes it happen?

From the rookie reporter, through the photographer, to the **Editor**, the newspaper is a hotbed of opportunity and talent. The industry also demonstrates the skills of printers and those who develop new technology to give us the news with increasing speed and clarity. We shall be looking at these jobs and others, with guidance for those who are interested in working in the world of the newspaper.

Where does it happen?

Newsgathering takes place anywhere where the action is. But deciding on the best story, the most effective way to put it across and how it will look on the page all takes place in the office. We shall be looking at where stories begin, where they end up and how modern technology has enabled the Editor to get them into print faster than ever before.

Will they last?

Newspaper companies and **news agencies** have been at the forefront of the **digital** revolution in newsgathering – providing on-line **copy** for the Internet and establishing their own websites. They have utilized television, developing teletext services. But what lies ahead for the printed page? We will be looking at how newspapers have to compete with a growing number of news services in the revolutionary age of information technology.

This impressive building belongs to The Observer newspaper in London. Newspapers are a multi-billion pound industry worldwide. They are financed not only by their cover price, but also, more importantly, through advertising. Pleasing the advertisers can at times affect the content of a newspaper and the way it is written.

Spoilt for choice

There is a huge choice of newspapers, ranging from local to national, **tabloid** to **broadsheet**, minority interest to global. Who wants to read them?

Papers for places

International, national, regional and local newspapers all published within one country compete for our loyalty. But each fulfils a different function, giving an international, national, regional or local flavour to the content. Most will also provide us with the major topical stories, which are more or less the same whichever paper you pick up on a particular day.

You will sometimes find newspapers from other countries on your local news-stand, especially if you live in a large city. News from superpowers, such as the USA, helps people working in finance, technology and other fields to pick up the trends and developments of their colleagues and rivals overseas.

Some papers cover regions that cross international boundaries, reflecting political or economic alliances. There are now, for instance, several European publications in different languages that cover the fifteen member states of the European Union (EU). This European organization decides a wide range of economic and social legislation. Newspapers seek to inform individual nation members of new developments and the effects they will have on member states.

*Community newspapers are run largely by local volunteers, and most of the **features** are written by local residents. These newspapers keep people in touch with what is happening on their own doorstep, such as this tree-planting event in Nepal.*

What's it all about?

When and where a newspaper is published affects the content of the paper. The time, place and content in turn are dependent on the demands of the readers. A rural weekly, for instance, is more likely to contain in-depth developments in agriculture and the environment. A national daily, on the other hand, will be focused on national and international headlines and finance. The newspaper proprietor (owner) has to provide for their primary readership, wherever that may be.

When do newspapers run? Some newspapers are published daily, with an early and a late **edition**, which reflects how quickly news items can change. Some dailies only publish in the evening. Weeklies are usually either a round-up of the week's news or cover specialist topics such as sport, finance or technology.

Special effects

Specialist topics normally lend themselves to the magazine style and format, but the cheapness and immediacy of **newsprint** have been chosen in certain circumstances. London's *New Musical Express* is the most popular pop music magazine in the UK, and yet it has the look and feel of a normal newspaper – not the glossy, glamorous appearance you might expect of a music publication. This has given the paper a casual, trendy image. Cost is a huge consideration for many organizations wishing to issue a publication – and again, cost is often related to image as well as money. If a local council wishes to promote its services, it often does so through a newspaper or news-sheet. This shows that it is not wasting the taxpayer's money on a lavish full-colour magazine or pamphlet!

This newspaper stand has been set up at an airport. News-stands are usually strategically placed outside subway stations or near taxi ranks to catch as much of the early morning trade as possible. Some countries produce national newspapers of two sizes. The smaller edition is called a tabloid, and the larger one, a broadsheet. The tabloids are much easier to handle, and are often written in a more straightforward style.

Around the world – cities and circulation

Every country produces a core of daily national newspapers, produced mostly in their major cities. Circulation, which means how many papers are sold, varies widely in different countries, even those with the same population total. A nation's literacy levels and ease of distribution affects the number of newspapers sold.

Papers for the people

Newspapers cost very little to buy, and with all the information packed inside are real value for money. They can even be passed on to someone else, making them a very economical read. These factors, plus the ready availability, are largely responsible for the newspaper's popularity in countries all over the world, whether rich or poor.

Most national daily papers are produced as well as read in a country's capital city or city state. Here, many of the most important stories take place, as capital cities are also a nation's political and financial centre. They are also where fashion, music and other cultural trends begin – and end. There is an instant readership for the newspaper, and a ready supply of businesses to help finance the paper through advertising.

This news item, about a fire in a backpackers' hostel, happened in the Australian state of Queensland. Many large nations are split up into states or regions, which are served by their own newspapers. In Australia, for instance, the Advertiser *focuses on news in South Australia.*

In the USA, the hub of the national newspaper industry is not Washington DC, the capital city, but New York City, which produces a large percentage of the USA's most popular newspapers. New York is the world's financial capital, and New York City is one of the most lively metropolitan centres. *The New York Times*, the *New York Daily News* and the *Wall Street Journal* each have a circulation of close to two million.

Countdown

There are fewer newspapers in the USA today than there were in 1900, when dailies numbered 2326. This is also true of many other countries in the economically advantaged world, where national, rather than local papers are having to fight for their circulation. Some of the reasons for this include how newspapers are financed and competition from other media. But there is also an increasing apathy toward political debate, traditionally one of the main topics for the national newspaper. Many people now want to be entertained by their daily, rather than informed.

As you can see from the table below, Kenya in East Africa has a large population, but only a small proportion of it reads its five national daily newspapers. This is due partly to Kenya's large dispersed rural population, its difficult road and rail communications, its literacy problems and its huge diversity of languages. But like most African nations, Kenya produces some robust journalism.

In the economically developing world and in countries with restricted political freedom, newspapers often flourish. Here in Nigeria, people are crowding around a newspaper seller.

Circulation

This table shows how popular or accessible daily newspapers are in different parts of the world.

Country	Population	No. of daily newspapers	Daily Circulation
USA	275 million	1483	56 million copies
UK	59 million	177	20 million copies
Australia	19 million	60	6 million copies
France	59 million	112	13 million copies
Kenya	30 million	5	300,000 copies

Around the world – a question of language

Literacy is a crucial factor in the popularity of the newspaper. But for a nation's newspaper industry, several languages being spoken in one country provides a challenge to reach as much of the population as possible.

One nation, many languages

We saw on page 6 that you will sometimes see newspapers from other countries on the news-stand. But some nations produce their own newspapers in different languages, to reflect the fact that they have more than one officially recognized tongue. Official languages are used in government, legislation, public notices and road signs, and are taught in schools. Some countries have several official languages. Switzerland, for example, uses French, German and Italian. Their newspapers are published in these languages, too.

Many countries in Africa and Asia were once occupied by other countries, such as France and Great Britain. These generally use French and English as one of their official languages, and a widely-used traditional language as another. So newspapers in Kenya, for instance, are published in either English or Swahili. The main dailies are the *Standard*, the *Daily Nation* and *Taifa Leo*, which means 'The Nation Today'.

Reaching the people

With its population of over 1.2 billion, China is a newspaper proprietor's dream in terms of circulation potential. **Communist** China's news publications are all controlled by the state and they are distributed to as many people as possible. The Chinese government also makes sure that in some regions, newspapers are published in several languages. This is so that China's ethnic minorities will be as well informed about government policies, technical and medical developments and so on, as the majority of the population.

The written Chinese language itself has also been simplified, making newspapers easier to read. The traditional written language is based on complex characters or word pictures. These have been slimmed down by using fewer strokes, while at the same time, a shorthand has been developed. In 1956 traditional characters were **romanized** to make them easier to learn and read. The new transcription is known as Pinyin. It uses the same letters as the words on this page. Foreign journalists working in China find it easier for writing names of places and people.

法神父指證小米特蘭走私
曾通知前總統夫人以圖

（本報巴黎訊）最受法國人尊敬以濟貧活動而揚名的彼耶神父，在昨（十九）日周五刊登的《費加羅日報》報道中披露，他曾經通知已故總統米特蘭的遺孀丹妮，有關其長子尚克里斯托夫在非洲的「若干活動」。並告知這位前第一夫人，「這樣會有不好的下場」，而請她「做一些事」補救。丹妮已透過律師接觸《費加羅日報》，聲稱彼耶神父從來沒有與她，談過尚克里斯托夫在非洲的活動。

這位神父向《費加羅日報》透露，一九

得接近前剛果總統莫布圖的兩名神父通知，父指尚克里斯托夫在莫布圖身邊，生活十分奢侈與排場闊綽。尤其是他們指責小米特蘭，火在出售軍火給安哥拉，而獲得大筆金錢利益。根據兩名剛果神父的說法，安哥拉將這些軍火轉售到盧旺達，當時這個國家正在爆發慘絕人寰的大屠殺悲劇。

提起與米特蘭遺孀的秘密約會，彼耶神父講述他們的會晤時指出，他曾向丹妮講述以下事情：出於友好的動機，有人要求他通知她，有關其子在非洲的若干活動。人們同剛

知她，有關其子在非洲的若干活動。人們同

This is part of an article in a Chinese newspaper published in the United Kingdom for Chinese readers. You need to learn about 3000 characters to be able to read a newspaper.

Spreading the news

It is estimated that about 500 million people read one of the world's 60,000 newspapers each day. About 33 per cent of all newspapers are published in North America, 33 per cent in Europe and 33 per cent in the rest of the world. On average, one person in every ten reads a daily newspaper. But there are vast areas of the world where the newspaper just cannot reach.

Setting the Scene

Calling the tune

Who runs the newspapers and how are they paid for? Newspapers are a cut-throat business, encouraging price wars and aggressive marketing to secure a share of the market. Good circulation figures encourage advertisers, who help keep newspapers in business.

Paper chains

Most of today's major newspapers are owned by huge corporations and media companies, which usually run a chain of newspapers. Today, very few national papers are truly independent. They cannot afford to be, as newspapers are very labour-intensive and costly to run. So a newspaper that is bought by a chain generally flourishes, as more money can be **invested** in it. It can also share news, printing and distribution networks with other papers in the chain. The management of the chain makes sure that each newspaper fills a particular gap or niche in the market so that it does not compete with other papers within its own chain.

In the USA, 20 major newspaper corporations run over half of all the daily circulation. One of the largest chains is Gannett Co. which owns over 90 papers, with a circulation of more than six million. In the UK and Australia, regional newspapers serving smaller cities and towns are often grouped together, too, within a particular geographical area.

Rupert Murdoch

Rupert Murdoch (born 1931 in Australia) is one of the world's most well-known multimedia bosses. He began his career by increasing the circulation of the family-owned newspaper, the *Adelaide News*, before setting up Australia's first national newspaper, *The Australian*. He went on to buy **tabloid** newspapers in both the USA and Great Britain. As a contrast with the sensationalism and populist image of these papers, Murdoch bought London's more serious *The Times* and *The Sunday Times* in 1981.

Making it pay

All newspapers have to be profitable, even if they are backed by a major company. Profits are made through advertising, receipts from the cover price (money received from customers buying the newspaper) and by selling the newspaper's own stories, **features** and photographs to other papers and media. Many regional and local newspapers have a greater circulation than nationals – but their reports and findings have less impact and they cannot attract as much advertising from big brand names as nationals. Free local newspapers are loaded with advertisements, with not a lot of news items. But research suggests that some people read newspapers only for their advertisements, so this is not a problem!

Who's the boss?

Newspaper owners or proprietors usually employ publishers or directors, who are responsible for the profitability of the newspaper. The publisher and the Editor-in-chief, sometimes called the Editorial-page editor, or even just **Editor**, are expected to make sure that the proprietor's basic political views are reflected in the paper. For small newspapers, the proprietor might be the publisher or director too, and occasionally also the Editor!

*Newspapers undertake their own **market research** to discover the kind of reader that will buy their paper. They question individuals, or **focus groups** drawn from their readership – the kind of people they believe will want to buy their paper. Circulation figures, though, are usually obtained, or at least verified, by independent organizations that newspapers can trust.*

On the job

A proprietor of a national newspaper is usually a very wealthy business person, often with interests in other media. But money is not everything. A proprietor of any type of newspaper, however small, has to have a good head for business and a keen sense of the newspaper and multimedia market. He or she must know how to finance a paper, so they have to understand their readership and advertising clientele.

Behind the scenes

A newspaper office simply buzzes with energy. Everyone has to work very closely with each other. Each person knows exactly what job they have to do and who to report to before an article is passed or a picture chosen.

Paper people

A major daily newspaper has a staff of over 100 reporters, editors, photographers and administrative personnel. While each paper is run slightly differently, the basic working structure is very similar, and it is managed very much like any other company. For most large outfits, management is headed by the publisher, or proprietor, who employs an **Editor** to help create and maintain **editorial policy** and oversee the smooth running of the news department. The Editor, together with the deputy and assistant editor and night editor, choose and pull together the stories and give the newspaper its flavour. Advertising and circulation managers form the basis of the business management team.

Down to work

All the managers work with assistants, or deputies, who make sure that policy decisions are carried out and deadlines met by the rest of the staff. One of the most important layers in this newsroom structure is occupied by the **copy-tasters**. They read and select the reports and articles that flood into the office from the reporters. This is a very important job, for choosing the wrong story or missing out on a **scoop** can lead to heavy criticism. While deputy editors and copy-tasters make sure that the stories are coming in and are being written along the right tracks, the **sub-editors**, or **copy editors**, wait to **edit** the reporters' **copy**.

You can see from these different sections of the Chicago Tribune *that many specialist reporters and editors are needed on major* **broadsheet** *newspapers. This paper sells over 600,000 copies each day.*

This is a typical open-plan newspaper office all on one floor. Easy communication is one of the key factors in a successful newspaper. The computers are linked so that a story can be easily put on screen for copy-editing and designing.

On the ground

A newspaper is nothing without its huge team of reporters, or journalists. In the city, many newspaper offices employ special city and city-suburb reporters, known in the USA as **metros**. These are supervised in the newsroom by a metro editor. The rest of the nation is covered by other reporters, some of whom specialize in urban issues, and others in rural affairs. Major newspapers also have bureaux – smaller satellite offices – in the major capitals of the world, staffed by foreign correspondents. Specialist reporters, supervised by section editors, cover finance, sport, the arts and entertainment, legal affairs, fashion and other interests, depending on the aims and structure of the newspaper.

While reporters are out researching and writing their stories, photographers and cartoonists are busy illustrating them, and the designers (including artists) are **laying them out** for clarity and the best visual effect. The advertising department is busy selling space.

On the job

The Editor moulds, and makes sure everyone keeps to, the style of the paper – both how it reads and how it looks. To be successful, the Editor has to know the newspaper's readership and be in tune with what it wants and the changes in its attitudes. Responding to the changes in society and the way people react to them is the key to keeping a readership happy.

All in a Day's Work

What's the story?

At the editorial conference, the **Editor** sets out the diary – the day-by-day schedule of jobs for the reporters. The diary outlines forthcoming **features** for specialist reporters. But there are always unexpected stories for the reporter to chase up.

Miniature tape recorders are a common interviewing tool. Tape recorders help reporters to concentrate on the interviewee and the questions they want to ask, although notebooks are also frequently used.

Reporting for duty

Who finds the stories? Most large newspapers employ at least 50 reporters. Most are staff reporters, which means that they work for the newspaper on a regular basis and are paid a salary. They are sent out to cover both pre-planned assignments and sudden headline-grabbers. Most are general reporters, covering a wide range of stories, while a few are specialists.

News editors also employ freelancers, who are only paid for the particular assignment for which they are hired. Freelancers often work for more than one newspaper, or for **news agencies**, and are ready to dash to the right spot when something interesting is happening. A good story, well-written, can be sold to the highest bidder, especially if it is an exclusive – one that no other journalist has reported. But it is the regular staff reporter who usually makes the big **scoop**, as they are part of a well-informed network of reporters, with a wide range of contacts.

Off to work

Once the diary has been sorted out, section editors brief their reporters so that they know exactly what they are going to be covering on a particular day or night. Some of these are the reporters with regular specialist assignments – covering reviews of films or plays, or motor shows, for instance. These stories are known as features.

Reporters often cover a particular part of a town or city, or an aspect of it, such as the courts and the city council. They concentrate mainly on important police cases, council meetings, the press conferences of big companies, or government initiatives. While there, they might be able to take advantage of a sudden scoop. This, though, is often the job of reporters on general assignment, who are asked to react to sudden news, such as a natural disaster.

Other reporters are investigative. They receive a small snippet of information, either from their editorial department or their own sources and then often spend many weeks getting to the bottom of it. This in-depth, painstaking reporting is often what leads to front-page revelations of, for instance, corruption in government. When a big story does **break**, it often sparks off a series of other revelations and consequences. In this case, the original scoop becomes what is called a 'running story'.

Reporters normally have to ask questions in a systematic manner and develop techniques to get their interviewee's confidence. But politicians are often pressed with the same question time and time again.

On the job

A reporter needs a very good command of English, a feel for what people want to read about and how different kinds of story can be best presented. He or she also has to be hungry for real information. Most reporters these days have a qualification in journalism – and many learn shorthand, which helps them write down information fast. A reporter's first job is usually as a local reporter, or 'stringer'.

First find the facts

The reporter has to be well organized and approach every story in the same professional manner. This means beginning with thorough background research, getting the facts right and noting them down in a systematic way.

Step by step

All types of assignment for a reporter require information to be gathered methodically, as this helps the reporter to write the story logically, accurately and quickly. It also enables them to check back on their story if any of the facts are questioned. Researchers often help with the initial fact finding.

A relatively simple story for a reporter on a national daily, for example, might be an official visit by a foreign premier (head of government). The reporter would first find background information about the country and the premier, then try to discover the reason for the visit. The reporter's first stop would be the country's prominent embassy staff to get the official line, and more secret inside sources to get the unofficial line. An established reporter would also have built up contacts in their own country's department of external affairs and possibly among members of that foreign country's community living abroad.

Once the premier arrives, the reporter attends press conferences and collects **press releases**. Depending on instructions from the **Editor**, the visit could be reported in the paper on a day-to-day basis, or as a single **feature** once the leader has returned home. This is unless the story develops an unexpected twist. Whatever the outcome, the reporter would be expected to come to some conclusion about the reason for the visit, its success or failure, and what it means for both countries, and possibly other parts of the world, in the long term.

A well-organized press conference allows a wide range of journalists to ask questions. All of the reporters take careful notes of the other journalists' questions, and the answers given, to help them construct their own story.

Background research

The reporter's story has to answer the following questions: Who? What? Where? When? Why? How? To do this, he or she first has to find out background information about a topic and whether or not there have been any other interesting stories surrounding it in the past. He or she might begin their research into a place, personality or event by using up-to-date yearbooks, the newspaper's own **archive** of back **issues**, and websites, such as CNN (Cable News Network). The reporter has now built up a basic picture. He or she can develop on this, by consulting personal contacts to get a deeper insight into specific aspects of the story.

Technical tips

A reporter has to make detailed notes from all their sources, giving a name, date, time and place for each one. This helps the reporter to write the story quickly, and enables them to refer back to the notes if the Editor queries any information or the source itself. The reporter has to follow a certain routine when they interview their contacts. They should have their questions well-prepared and must not try to manipulate the answer. After the story has been printed, the reporter might also be asked to verify facts in a court of law. If their notebook is well organized they can instantly call upon a fact, a name, a date and a place. Tape-recorded interviews are still less respected by courts than the reporter's notebook.

In the UK, the question of who should run the National Lottery is treated differently by the **broadsheet** *newspaper (left) and the* **tabloid**. *For a serious political story, a tabloid highlights the main points and makes a splash with anything that is even slightly sensational. A broadsheet will give more detailed background, a longer, more systematic development of the story, and usually a more balanced conclusion.*

Writing it down

Once the story has been investigated, the reporter gets down to writing it. Well-researched and clearly written notes make the task much easier. But the reporter still has to make the story clear and keep to the newspaper's writing style. Then it has to be sent to the office.

Taking and tasting

*The copy-taker listens to the reporter through headphones and types the story straight into the computer. The software enables the story to be taken down more or less in the correct format, so that it is easy for the designer to **lay it out** (see page 36).*

A very experienced reporter is able to dictate their story down a telephone line to a **copy-taker**. But on the whole, stories are typed on computer, either at home, in the office or on the move. Roving reporters can use laptops with fold-down screens. All these machines are linked to computer terminals in the newspaper office, where the report is saved on a **server**. This enables all the other people working on the article to call it up on a computer screen so that they can work on it. Whichever way the reporter sends the story to the office, he or she has to make it clear who wrote it and to give the story itself a catchline. This is so that anyone who requires access to it can call it up on screen.

All stories go first to the **copy-taster**, who sorts out the stories into different subject areas and rejects those that are not suitable. Not all the stories are accepted, even though the reporters might have been asked to write them. These 'dead' stories are stored on the 'spike' – which was once a library of catalogued, typed reports, but nowadays is a computer file.

The right style

The reporter's job is to make the story clear by starting with the main action or point of the story to get the reader's attention. This is followed by details – the names of those involved, a time, date and place of the event and quotes from witnesses or experts. The story can be concluded with the consequences of what has happened, if these are known. The story must not be hidden in detail, which is why the main point of it is usually written up front. But if the story is very unusual or amusing, the reporter might lead up to it more slowly – a technique known as the delayed drop.

Reporters tend to write short sentences and avoid using long words where a shorter one will do. A reporter will sometimes be given a rough idea of how many words the story should contain, although it is always **edited** to a more precise length later by the **sub-editor**, also known as the **copy editor**. The reporter doesn't have to consider layout when the story is being written.

Sometimes, a report has to fit into a very small space at the end of a column. This is known as an end-column brief. Writing the main points of a story in a small space such as this requires great skill, although a good sub-editor can help to create a sharp, punchy report.

A **tabloid** story is very straightforward in style and uses language that tends to provoke the reader, while the **broadsheet** has a calmer, but often more complex style and uses more background information. A weekly newspaper, which, for example, is published on a Sunday, will not be able to create suspense in a story that hit the stands the previous Monday. It might therefore use the story briefly as part of a news round-up, or at length as a subject for analysis.

Before a reporter's story is passed by the news editor, the sub-editor makes sure that it will not break any law by passing anything suspicious to the paper's legal department. The reporter has to check that interviewees' names are used with their permission. Sub-editors check that the names of places and people are spelled accurately. The reporter's finished story is worked on by the sub-editor (or copy editor). He or she edits the story for length, known as casting off, and makes sure that it conforms to the paper's **house style**.

On the job

A sub-editor needs very good English and must be able to sort out information and rework it in a clear manner. He or she also needs an eye for detail and an ability to work to very tight deadlines without getting in a panic. Most sub-editors these days have a qualification in journalism and work their way up from local to national newspapers.

Tales from afar

Newsgathering abroad presents challenges both for the foreign correspondent and the newspaper office. Sometimes the paper will not be able to send their own reporter to the scene, so they have to rely on other sources of information.

Big stories abroad

Major newspapers set up bureaux in most of the world's capital cities. Their foreign correspondents enable us to read the stories behind overseas elections, global financial changes, natural disasters and so on, not only in the capitals, but over a wide area surrounding them. This is because a correspondent based, for example, in Beijing or Tokyo might also be responsible for newsgathering in other parts of the Far East.

A foreign correspondent uses the research facilities of its newspaper headquarters and communicates with them mostly now through e-mail and telephone, and occasionally fax. The reporter also develops contacts with local people and the reporter's own country's embassy staff. Most countries give foreign journalists the official line through government spokespersons. If an important story **breaks** in the USA, for instance, officials at the White House in Washington give out **press releases** to waiting journalists of all types of media.

*This is a Reuters press agency office in an extremely rare, quiet moment. While press agencies are useful sources of information, a newspaper is always aware that stories come second-hand, via reporters over whom they have no control. Once in the newspaper office, agency stories have to be rewritten according to the **house style**.*

Down to earth

Foreign correspondents do not only respond to the news that foreign governments want them to report. Many foreign correspondents are investigative, and try to uncover stories that they think the rest of the world should know about. This often means travelling outside the capital, where fewer people speak an international language. Correspondents often have to rely on translators to help them get to the bottom of a story. This, and cultural differences, can make getting to the truth very difficult.

Engaging the agencies

Foreign news sections sometimes cannnot get information on all the stories they need, and have to use the huge **news agencies**, which have hundreds of reporters, agents and statisticians all over the world. Many countries have an agency located in their capital. Associated Press and United Press International are the USA's largest. Reuters covers most of Europe plus Australia and New Zealand, while the UK's main agency is the Press Association. The last three, together with France's Agence France-Presse provide information for a circulation of over 450 million every day.

During China's Tiananmen Square disturbances in 1990, plain clothes policemen attacked foreign journalists, as you can see here. The Chinese government did not want stories of oppression to reach the rest of the world.

Ruling the news

Economically developing countries have long complained that the news and overall cultural flavour in its presentation is dominated by the rich western world. But the United Nations' attempt in the 1970s to make newsgathering more balanced through a New World Information Order was thrown out by rich nations. One of the Order's rejected recommendations was that journalists should obtain a licence before they could research and write a story.

The last word

The daily newspaper is made up of hundreds of different stories, a bit like a patchwork quilt. But someone has to pull them all together to give the newspaper its particular flavour. This is what makes it attractive to its readership. The person responsible is the **Editor**.

The Editor and their team solve problems and discuss ideas at a daily meeting. While the Editor has overall control, opinion is often shaped by the leader writer, who comments on current events in the leader column.

Mapping it out

The Editor guides both the content and presentation of the newspaper. He or she sometimes writes the **leader** column or other commentary columns, too. These highlight the paper's view on current stories or issues, and reflect the paper's political and social position. But the Editor's first job is to make sure that each **edition** runs smoothly and comes out on time, so he or she begins the day with a team meeting. As well as planning the stories and schedule at this meeting, the team usually discusses any issues surrounding the last edition.

During the day, the Editor, the deputy or the night editor (who sometimes substitutes for the Editor) is on hand to make sure that the most important stories are given prominence and that the schedule is being met. As news **breaks** and as the country and the world respond to it, the importance and emphasis of the day's stories tend to shift. Sometimes this means that items have to be moved further to the back of the newspaper and given less column space, while others are brought forward.

The Editor has to be aware of sudden headline-making stories. But this must not put back the schedule for the rest of the newspaper. Each page is given a slot – a time in which everything must be completed and checked. The Editor also usually has the last word on the choice of pictures, especially on the front page. These kinds of decisions are usually made at a production meeting later on in the day, where picture, news and **features** editors put forward their views.

Leading the way

The importance of the front pages, especially the headlines and photographs, lies in the way they set the image of the newspaper, which helps secure the paper's share of the market. Long-standing newspapers have a firm niche, developed by previous Editors and proprietors. This must be held by the existing Editor, and built upon.

However, Editors are probably as much influenced by circulation figures and advertising revenue as anything else – in other words their decisions are affected by making money. The Editor works increasingly closely with the advertising director and the promotions manager to attract the right kind of advertising for its readership. Most dailies now include more financial news to encourage business advertising, such as banks and insurance companies.

Using the news

In some countries governments are not **democratically** elected, and they have more control over newspaper editors. But it is still sometimes possible to publish quite a controversial subject, depending on how it is written and the editorial slant given. The government in turn often uses the Editor to inform the public about government policies, triumphs and so on. But this is not so very different from the **press releases** of democratically-elected governments, or stories put about by their premiers' **spin-doctors** or publicists.

Some stories are difficult to position in the newspaper until they have unfolded properly. This marathon might make the front page, but probably only if the winner comes from the country that the newspaper is published in, or if something unusual occurs along the way.

Seeing is Believing

Every picture tells a story

A front-page picture has to grab your attention, tell you instantly what is happening and create an atmosphere. In other words it must stand alone, without words to help it. Inside, pictures often just show the facts but do not pull on the emotions. A newspaper has to employ well-organized and talented photographers to achieve these goals.

Picture this ...

*The paparazzi follow, and occasionally mob, anyone who can make front-page news, especially in the **tabloids**. Here, the actress Julia Roberts is under the spotlight at a premier for the film Notting Hill.*

Newspapers mostly use staff photographers, but also take pictures from self-employed freelancers, who can sometimes pick up on sudden stories that a newspaper office might not have been able to react to in time. The staff photographer's day begins with a briefing from the picture editor who is sometimes also the chief photographer. Like reporters, each photographer is handed an assignment, which has been worked out jointly with the picture editor and the news editor. Like reporters, their first job is to find out as much about the place, event and the people involved as possible. Then they have to check their equipment, making sure they have the right type of film with the correct speed for day or night shooting, and spare flashbulbs and batteries.

The photographer has to go to the site, and if there is time, study angles and light sources, and make sure they know where the action is going to happen. An experienced photographer can take all this in in just a couple of minutes. But modern cameras help out when time is tight as they can take pictures in very quick succession. This enables the photographer to get plenty of images of something or someone moving quickly – very useful for celebrity photographers (paparazzi) trying to get a good shot of a reluctant star, or the very moment an earthquake begins to topple skyscrapers.

What are they looking for?

Every photographer wants a dazzling front-page news picture, so they have to be in the right place at the right time. But more than this, their picture editor and the news editor will be looking for a shot that captures the essence of the story, the mood, and that something extra – a different angle, maybe, or the perfect expression on someone's face. The picture has to be suitable for the style and image of the particular newspaper, too.

*Most professional newspaper photographers these days use either cameras which take 35 mm film or **digital** cameras. Digital photography allows pictures to be checked on a computer and then sent instantly down a phone line to the newsroom.*

On the job

A newspaper's staff photographer needs very good technical skills. He or she also needs a keen eye for composition (the way in which elements in a photo are arranged) and interesting angles – something that is partly instinctive and partly practice. A photographer must be able to assess quickly what equipment and position they need for each job. He or she must have a very good knowledge of current affairs and public personalities, just like a reporter.

The best view

The photographer now needs to get the pictures to the newsroom as quickly as possible. There the picture editor can sift out any images that are of poor quality. Then the important task of selection can begin.

Down the wire

If a photographer is using film, this is developed immediately. Then the photographer uses a scanner attached to a laptop with a **modem** to send the pictures down a telephone line to the Electronic Picture Desk (EPD). **Digital** cameras are now being used for instant accessibility. Images are stored on a chip and then transmitted straight to the Electronic Picture Desk monitor.

On the EPD screen, a whole batch of shots can be laid out in a series of rows that fill the screen, or the shots can be made into a single print known as a contact sheet. This makes it easier to compare all the images at once.

Size and disguise

With the help of the picture editor, the news, **features** or other editor selects the best shots, although the final decision for an important picture will rest with the **Editor** or night editor. But however good the final choice is, it is rare that a photographer can take a perfect picture that needs no cropping (cutting) or touching (removing blotches and blemishes). One of the most important reasons for cropping is so that the picture fits into the space intended for it. Cropping can also give the picture its punch by focusing on the most important or dramatic part – or leaving out a detail that might distract from the impact of the picture.

Looking good

Each developed film frame obviously has to be enlarged, just like holiday photographs. But the final image also has to be the same shape as the space that is left for it on the page, which is not necessarily the same as a 35 mm frame. So the picture has to be sized in proportion to the space available, and cropped. While most cropping and sizing is now undertaken on-screen, newspapers that are not fully computerized still crop black-and-white prints by hand.

In a fully-computerized system, the **edited** pictures are touched up on screen if necessary. Blobs and blemishes really show up on the printed page, so they are disguised by moving around some of the tiny **pixels** that make up the picture on the screen. This blends the blobs with their surrounding tone or colour. Once all the pictures have been chosen, sized and cropped they are sent from the EPD to the page-making terminals to be **laid out** by the designer, whose job we will find out about on page 36.

Cropping pictures can alter the message they give. Here, the full picture contrasts wealth with poverty and loneliness. The cropped picture shows only wealth and comfort.

Hunting for pictures

Newspapers also buy the **rights** to use pictures from agencies, or to download them from Internet picture libraries. Other images come from CD-ROMs, or stills from television, known as video-grabbed pictures. Most of the big newspapers and **syndicates** have their own libraries, too. Agencies often provide portraits of well-known people, used when something important happens to them – or when they die and are written about in the obituaries column.

More than News

Selling space

Advertisements help to pay for newspapers, and they often help to sell them, too. The advertising director has to make sure that the paper carries enough adverts and that they will attract the reader. In turn, good circulation figures help to pull in more advertisers.

Tele-ad salespeople use a rate card to tell their customers how much their advertisement will cost. Display ads are usually charged by the amount of space they take up, while classified ads are paid for by the number of words printed, plus any extra design features.

Attracting the business

Newspaper advertising is a multi-billion pound industry, and comes close to television advertising in the amount of money spent on it each year. Popular national **tabloid** newspapers need to fill about 40 per cent of each **issue** to help pay for the paper's production costs, while the more serious, but often slightly less popular, national **broadsheets** can require as much as 70 per cent. So it is no surprise that the advertising director is one of the most important of the newspaper personnel. The director and the advertising managers of different sections of the newspaper make sure that each area – from news, through finance, sport, women's pages and so on – has the correct amount and type of advertising.

In the offices, tele-ad salespeople have to sell the spaces allotted for each section. Outside, advertising reps are sent to encourage advertising from businesses within the particular area assigned to each of them. When all the advertisment deals have been struck, the ads are usually designed and **laid out** on the page by a separate team from the one producing the main newspaper sections.

The right type of ad

The wide distribution networks of the major papers encourage well-known goods and services to place their ads in all types of national newspaper. These are the large, sophisticated advertisements known as display ads. Placement of ads for big brand names such as Coca Cola or McDonald's is crucial. These have a very specific image, of youth and fun, so they do not want their ads to be placed, for instance, near the obituaries column!

Classified ads are the ones that the reader scours for bargain buys, holidays, cars and homes. They are classified, or categorized, according to the type of purchase being advertised, and there is often a specific day on which to look for particular items. Classified ads are where local and regional papers really come into their own. Local businesses are very keen to take advantage of these newspapers' good circulation to advertise. This is also true of the growing number of free papers, which are usually between 80 and 90 per cent advertisements.

Large brand-name newspaper ads form part of companies' publicity strategies, so you will see links between all types of advertising for a particular product. Small classified ads for goods such as homes and cars follow a set format, with abbreviations for words that everyone comes to recognize. They rarely have illustrations.

On the job

On a large newspaper, the advertising director works with the **Editor** and circulation manager to establish an advertising strategy that suits the finances and image of the newspaper. He or she has many contacts with the business world to help secure advertising contracts. The advertising director has to keep up to date with advertising trends and the changing images of companies wishing to advertise in his or her newspaper.

A little light relief

Newspapers are generally serious affairs. But the reader can always find something to entertain them. Politics has its amusing side, which is well exploited by the cartoonist, while crosswords, horoscopes and agony columns provide a healthy diversion to the gloom and doom.

The number and type of cartoons, crosswords, quizzes and so on often reflect the tone of a particular paper. The serious broadsheets usually include more, and deeper, political cartoons than the tabloid. There are usually no horoscopes or agony-aunt columns. These are the province of the tabloid press, which often also includes the latest stories of the stars.

A sense of humour

Readers have their own cartoon favourites, which bring a smile early in the day. There are three main types of cartoon. The political type targets the latest antics of politicians, and government decisions. Political cartoons are usually placed close to the column revealing the story they illustrate. The second type are regular comments by a particular cartoonist on news items, famous personalities, and again, politicians. But they are usually subtle, wry observations which link the news more with the average person's everyday challenges. These cartoons are usually **laid out** in a regular position – often on the front or inside-front pages. Finally, there is the strip cartoon, based on a character or set of characters. Some, such as the world-famous 'Peanuts' and 'Andy Capp' are miniature episodes in the characters' lives. They focus on the problems of life and relationships, often within the context of modern society.

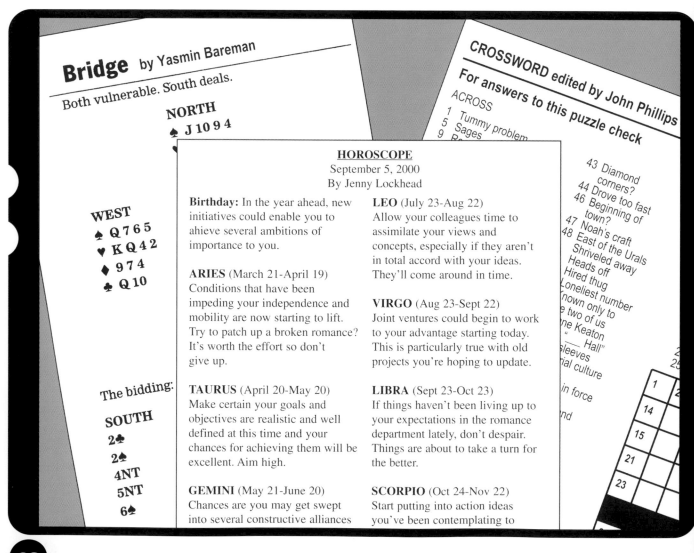

Bridge by Yasmin Bareman

Both vulnerable. South deals.

NORTH
♠ J 10 9 4

WEST
♠ Q 7 6 5
♥ K Q 4 2
♦ 9 7 4
♣ Q 10

The bidding:

SOUTH
2♣
2♠
4NT
5NT
6♣

CROSSWORD edited by John Phillips

For answers to this puzzle check

ACROSS
1 Tummy problem
5 Sages
9 R...

43 Diamond corners?
44 Drove too fast
46 Beginning of town?
47 Noah's craft
48 East of the Urals
   Shriveled away
   Heads off
   Hired thug
   Loneliest number
   Known only to
   the two of us
   ...ne Keaton
   "___ Hall"
   ...sleeves
   ...ial culture
   ...in force
   ...nd

HOROSCOPE
September 5, 2000
By Jenny Lockhead

Birthday: In the year ahead, new initiatives could enable you to achieve several ambitions of importance to you.

ARIES (March 21-April 19)
Conditions that have been impeding your independence and mobility are now starting to lift. Try to patch up a broken romance? It's worth the effort so don't give up.

TAURUS (April 20-May 20)
Make certain your goals and objectives are realistic and well defined at this time and your chances for achieving them will be excellent. Aim high.

GEMINI (May 21-June 20)
Chances are you may get swept into several constructive alliances

LEO (July 23-Aug 22)
Allow your colleagues time to assimilate your views and concepts, especially if they aren't in total accord with your ideas. They'll come around in time.

VIRGO (Aug 23-Sept 22)
Joint ventures could begin to work to your advantage starting today. This is particularly true with old projects you're hoping to update.

LIBRA (Sept 23-Oct 23)
If things haven't been living up to your expectations in the romance department lately, don't despair. Things are about to take a turn for the better.

SCORPIO (Oct 24-Nov 22)
Start putting into action ideas you've been contemplating to

The American cartoonist, Charles Schulz (1922-2000), created the most successful cartoon strip of all time in the clever, enchanting 'Peanuts'. His characters, although children (and Snoopy the dog!), demonstrated mature feelings and reactions towards quite adult problems. By the 1990s, the 'Peanuts' cartoon was enjoyed by 200 million people every day. It now appears in 2600 newspapers published in 75 countries. Schulz always drew all the cartoons himself.

Crosswords and cross words

Life's puzzles, and crossword puzzles, are often what we turn to first in our daily newspaper. Problem pages, often referred to as 'agony aunt' columns, blossomed in the 1960s, as worldy-wise women sought to solve in public the problems sent to them in private. On the whole, agony aunts try to sort out differences between people, but the issues, once quite mild and timeless, have become increasingly personal, and concern very complex dilemmas.

Crossword puzzles help the commuter to while away the time, or are a form of escapism during the worker's lunchbreak. Crossword compilers are very skilled and usually have a regular slot in a newspaper. The quick crossword requires only a one-word answer for each place. Cryptic crosswords are more complex – the solution must not only answer the clue but should at the same time be made up of individual parts of the clue itself. Some solutions are anagrams of a word or words in the clue. On the whole, **broadsheet** newspapers include more complex crosswords, and bridge and chess puzzles. **Tabloids** provide quick quizzes to reflect their lighter, brighter overall style.

After 'The Simpsons'

Matt Groening, the American creator of 'The Simpsons', began his career as a newspaper cartoonist. His cartoon strip 'Life in Hell' was first published in a small local newspaper, but was gradually bought up by others throughout the USA. Readers identified with the everyday problems, dilemmas and fears of the central character. Groening said in 2000, in an interview marking the tenth anniversary of 'The Simpsons', that he would like to make an animated version of 'Life in Hell'. Let's just hope!

Something for everyone

Not everyone wants to read just news stories or news **features**, and the occasional lift of a cartoon or puzzle are not enough to entertain today's reader. This is why, in the last 30 years, newspapers have devoted more space to special interest sections and lifestyle articles.

Extra special

Among the daily news, readers can expect to find special interest columns, pages, pull-outs and supplements. These cover a wide range of topics – sport, finance, the arts, other media, media personalities, food, fashion and travel. The **broadsheets**' presentation of the material is usually as sophisticated as their news sections, but lighter in tone and brighter in presentation, while the **tabloids** usually go for their more up-beat, popular style. Broadsheets tend to analyse trends more than the tabloids, which seek to spark interest in, say, fashion, home decoration and travel through the lifestyles and opinions of the stars.

Through newspaper supplements, lifestyle, entertainment, sport and travel have become linked, even though each topic can be read in separate sections. Journalists for supplements follow individual trends for each subject, pull them all together and create a lifestyle 'culture'. This changes when there is a new fashion in, say, home-decorating materials or travel destinations. In fact, a new trend in travel destinations often sparks off changes in other lifestyle slots. For example, a fashion for North African holidays leads to an interest in North African architecture, furniture, gardens, cuisine, materials and their colours. The supplement or pull-out is perfect for pulling all these together. Supplements can sometimes even begin new trends that are taken up by other media and designers.

Is this advertising?

Because they encourage people to go out and buy the latest goods, or take part in the current exercise trend, supplements and lifestyle articles are known as consumer journalism or service columns. They come very close to being advertisement features when they compare certain products. There is a fine line to be drawn between discussing trends by referring to certain products, and openly advertising the product itself.

Catching up

Saturday and Sunday newspapers provide a round-up of the week's events, enabling busy people to catch up with the news as well as taking in the latest headlines. Buyers of weekend broadsheets expect to find deeper analysis of political, social and economic affairs, but also items on entertainment. Weekend tabloid readers expect more news stories plus a lot more showbiz and sport information. Readers of both types of newspaper also look forward to the many additional supplements.

Some weekend papers are allied to dailies as their linked titles suggest, although different **Editors** and other managerial staff are employed for each. Editors for these weekend papers are often very high-profile journalists and political and social commentators. Other weekend papers are independent of any daily, although they may be part of the same stable (group of newspapers).

The idea of weekend papers began in the UK in the late 18th century, but was not taken up on a large scale until the mid-20th century. Then, the USA powered the way with a whole range of weekend newspapers and supplements. In the UK, the first weekend paper was launched under the progressive proprietor, Lord Thomson. *The Sunday Times* became a sister edition to London's famous *The Times*.

Stick to the news!

Journalists writing lifestyle features are usually different from those writing news items. Many of these are concerned that supplement articles actively encourage readers to buy certain goods or services. Journalists' trades unions have worked hard to ensure that advertising support material does not openly endorse products and that the newspaper is not open to pressure by advertisers. Most newspapers now make sure that advertisement features are subtitled as such.

Lifestyle sections follow times of the year as well as trends. This helps to give the material focus, and enables it to be more easily planned. Here, readers' minds are turned towards next year's holiday and the designer Guy Laroche shows his 1998/1999 winter collection in Paris.

Putting it Together

Laying it out

The design of a newspaper has to attract its readers and maintain a style that reflects the tone of the newspaper. It also has to contain all the information that the reader expects. This artistic jigsaw puzzle all has to be achieved at great speed, too!

Looking good

A newspaper can be planned, designed and **laid out** on computer, although a few newspaper designers, together with the major editors, like to plan it out on paper first. One of the first stages is the rough, or scheme, which is an outline of the page layouts. These give the basic dimensions within which the designer and editors have to work. Spaces are then blocked out to allow for known display ads, regular **feature** columns, crosswords, cartoons and so on, leaving the rest to be filled in. The night editor and the chief **sub-editor** choose the headline stories and then roughly key them into the front, inside-front and, in the case of the **tabloid**, the centre pages. These are the areas of most concern to the **Editor**.

When the day's news comes rolling in, the rough is sent to the designer or artist. He or she works with assistants to size the spaces for illustrations and **copy** so that they can give a more definite set of layouts, or flat plans. These have to be passed by the editors in charge before they are handed on to the sub-editors (subs). The subs then **edit** the stories and features on screen so that the lettering, or setting, fits the layouts. Each column width is set, or justified, and as the sub keys in the text, it automatically fits that width. However, this sometimes leads to uneven spacing between words, which then have to be adjusted, or kerned. The photos and **artwork** are scaled – or sized (see page 28) – and the design is complete.

Each page of a **broadsheet** newspaper usually measures about 38 x 58 centimetres (15 x 23 inches), while tabloids are about 28 x 38 centimetres (11 x 15 inches). It has always been more difficult to design the tabloid, as space is tight and the demands for bigger, bolder headlines greater than those of the broadsheet. But flexible computer design software has enabled designers to solve this dilemma.

Designers and editors use their skills to make sure that some stories receive more prominence than others. Some are given a special **typeface** and style so that they stand out. These stories are known as splashes. Plainer, straighter sans serif typefaces are used mostly in tabloids while curlier, serif faces are more broadsheet style. But most stories show their strength by their headline, which helps the reader to easily prioritize and select what they want to read as they flick quickly through a newspaper.

Technical tips

Typefaces are measured using points. Each point is tiny – about three points make up a millimetre in length. To measure a typeface, the distance is taken between the top of an ascending letter, such as an 'h' and the bottom of a descending letter, such as 'g'. The letters in this book are in 11 point, but you need a special points' rule in order to measure them.

A really major headline is set in a huge, bold, plain typeface. These are known disaster caps. Another dramatic headline design is to print white letters on a black background – or WOB (white on black) – while a banner headline spans the whole width of the page.

The 'bomb' headline, laid out in three lines, is the second most important story of the day and is known as the half head. Small headlines such as 'Sportstime' are usually placed in the bottom half of the paper where the 'filler' stories are laid out.

Bomb kills 9 in Moscow

Blast goes off in underground walkway

Sportstime

Sun worshippers who

FIRE HORROR

Four die in stayover at gran's

Crowds still basking in guilty pleasure

Hot off the press

A whole newspaper, with all the type, layout and photographic instructions can now be keyed or scanned into a computer. Computer software then translates the information to pages made of film negative, which in turn is transferred to machinery that makes metal printing plates. It is the inked plates that eventually put print onto the paper. All this can be done in just one building complex.

Putting it on paper

Most newspapers these days, whether local, regional or national, use web-offset machines to print their papers. But first, all the stories, pictures and advertisements held in the computer are decoded and the pages made into negative film. Each page is then transferred by a very bright light to a fine, photo-sensitive plate, coated in a synthetic rubbery substance called a polymer, which takes the shape of the text and pictures as the strong light burns out the unwanted polymer surrounding it. The plate is then dipped in a tank of ink, and the wet, inked polymer words and pictures then stamp a cylinder covered with a rubberised coating. It is the cylinder that prints the text and pictures onto cheap, coarse paper, known as **newsprint**. Transferring the print from one surface to another is called offsetting – hence the name of the printing machine.

A splash of colour

Colour is now used widely in newspapers, thanks to electronic scanning. Colour cannot be printed without first separating out the four colours that together make up the different hues in a picture – cyan, yellow, cerise and black. The electronic scanner enables positive prints and **artwork** to be used, not just colour **transparencies**, which was all the old scanners could manage. This has speeded up the process, as the prints and artwork don't have to be photographed first before they are scanned. Once the colours have been separated out, each sheet of paper has to be rolled through the press four times to pick up the four coloured inks in turn. This obviously takes longer than ordinary black print, which is why particular pages are always set aside for colour, while the majority of the paper gets printed.

Spreading the news

Computerization has enabled newspapers to be published as several different **editions** at once, for different parts of a city, region, country or even the world. The USA's *Wall Street Journal*, for instance, prints four regional editions every day. The technology that allows this is the **facsimile**. This is not the fax machine, which can only transmit printed paper, sheet by sheet, but scanners which first read and then shrink the written, design and printing information of a whole newspaper held on a **server**. Once shrunk in **digital** form, it can be sent down telephone lines to a local printing press. Here, a computer translates the code back into the original information and instructions, which are then followed by the local scanning and printing machines.

Web-offset machines have certainly speeded up newspaper printing. But there are downsides to the system. The machinery is expensive to buy and maintain, and it wastes more newsprint than older print equipment, such as rotary presses. This is why it took some major national newspapers 20 years to change to web-offset. The first to take advantage of the new technology were regional and local newspapers in the USA.

The price of progress

Technical innovation has led to a huge reduction in the time it takes to print a newspaper. But it has encouraged overproduction of newspapers and has also led to massive job losses in the print industry. In 1986, the newspaper tycoon Rupert Murdoch built a high-technology printing plant at Wapping in London, to serve his UK newspapers. There were massive protests from the printers' and journalists' unions, but they failed to stop the 'progress'.

On the stands

The printed papers, literally 'hot' off the press, are bundled and strapped, usually by machine. Then they are stacked in a warehouse and despatched to various parts of the city or region. There are several ways in which a reader can get hold of a copy.

The early bird

Newspaper offices and printing presses are usually very close to their central distribution points – sometimes in the same building complex. This is essential, as newspapers need to be on the stands and in the shops as the first early-morning commuters start out for work. Vans transport the latest **edition** to local distribution companies. There are usually only one or two of these in each town or city, holding papers from several different chains. From the distribution points, newspapers are delivered to newsagents, news-stands and outlets in bus and train stations, and airports. Many governments try to encourage newspaper sales – in the USA, newspapers have special mailing rates which helps keep the cover price down and encourages readership.

As we saw on page 38, the use of the **facsimile** for transmitting news **copy digitally**, has replaced transportation of finished copies by train and plane to the far corners of a country. In vast nations such as the USA and Australia, though, time changes mean that national newspapers are transmitted earlier in some parts of the country than others.

Here, newspapers are being delivered to a news stand in New York City, USA. Back at the newspaper office, vans are being prepared to transport more newspapers to other to distribution points. The vans are often marked with the newspaper's title or company.

We're running out!

What you will see in the shops is a full range of **broadsheet** and **tabloid** first editions. When these run out, the shopowner has to ring through to the local distribution point for more copies of particular papers. Sometimes readers have to wait until deliveries of the later edition are made. It is just as difficult for the newsagent to calculate the number of papers it needs each day as it is for the newspaper to assess the correct number of copies to be printed. A sudden **scoop** by one newspaper will entice readers away from their usual title and quickly run down the supply. At the newspaper office, the circulation manager, together with the editor-in-charge, has to estimate the number of copies needed according to the response they think they will get to the lead and half-lead news stories.

Stop press!

In the face of litigation (legal action) or government outrage, **Editors** very occasionally have to print a newspaper with a blank column, sometimes accompanied by a blank space for the picture that goes with it. But mostly, last minute changes are all about putting new material in rather than taking it out. A sudden newsflash means that, if possible, the newspaper has to add the story to a 'late news' section, known as a fudge, either on the front or the back page. The word 'fudge' comes from 'fudge box', a system used in the days of the hot metal press for inserting late news. Modern newspaper computer systems can quickly update last-minute facts and figures, such as sports results, which can be added at a very late stage.

Newsagents are often organized in chains, just like distributors and newspaper companies. They are able to offer a wider choice of newspapers than small, independent newsagents.

New places for papers

Newspaper Editors and circulation managers are always trying to find different outlets for their papers. In recent years these have included supermarkets and petrol stations. When a newspaper collaborates with an organization, such as a tourist office, to produce a special pull-out or supplement, that office can also be used as a sales point. The big question is whether or not including commercial material in this way alters the balance of the paper's content in favour of advertising and service columns (see pages 30 and 34).

Under Pressure

Was it right? Was it fair?

Newspapers have to print accurate information or they can end up being prosecuted for libel. Libel is the act of writing something wrong and harmful about a person or group of people. But it can also be unlawful to publish details of people's private lives. These laws vary from one country to another.

Laying down the law

The issue of press freedom is continually under scrutiny. In countries ruled by powerful dictators and under **communist** regimes, both journalists and the public see their struggle for press freedom as a battle for human rights. In more **democratic** countries, **Editors** still challenge governments over policies and cover-ups. When a government orders a newspaper not to publish a particular story, Editors may pointedly publish front pages with blank columns to highlight the fact that they have been censored. At other times they write the forbidden story cleverly, in consultation with their own libel lawyers and legal editors.

When a newspaper Editor wishes to publish an important rumour, rather than a confirmed **scoop**, the story is worded very carefully. We often read, 'It is reported that ...', 'It is alleged that ...', 'It is rumoured that ...' or 'An unnamed source stated that ...', rather than a direct statement from an actual source. This often prevents the newspaper from being prosecuted. But does it give us news, or just 'no-story' stories that leave us with very little idea of what is really happening? These kind of reports are increasing in the face of huge competition for circulation.

Journalists are rarely able to report disasters openly and fully, such as this aircraft accident at Fukuoka airport in Japan. This is partly because it takes a long time to find out the causes and effects of disasters, and partly because companies or governments do not want people to lose confidence in them.

Following the code

In most countries, newspapers are expected to abide by a code of conduct negotiated between journalists, press organizations and government representatives. These codes usually try at the very least to protect children and vulnerable people, as these groups are unable to protect themselves against press intrusion. In the last decade, in the UK, journalists have been accused of reluctance to agree to privacy rights for other individuals. But in 1993 it was finally agreed that the public should have access to a helpline, so that infringements of individuals' rights could be reported and investigated.

This person is trying to protect himself from publicity while he attends court proceedings. But there is nothing stopping photographers from taking your picture. It will usually only get printed, though, if the newspaper's lawyers know that it is legal to do so.

Hiding the truth

During the Gulf War and the war in Bosnia, journalists from the USA and European countries were restricted by governments on both sides of the conflict. Reporters were allowed by their own governments only to report official statements made by military personnel and defence departments. Journalists based in Baghdad and Belgrade had their stories read and **censored** by the authorities. On both sides, this was deemed necessary in order to 'protect lives'.

The verdict and future trends

Newspapers continue to find a place for themselves in the face of fierce competition from radio, television and the Internet. What keeps people interested in **newsprint**? What keeps them loyal to the medium?

Finding a place

Radio, television and now the Internet challenge newspapers as the major information medium. So how can the newspaper keep its place in the face of new information technology? To a certain extent, newspapers have extended their own lives by helping to develop teletext and Internet news services. These have the potential to extend news stories, update them or lay them out in bullet points so that they are easy to catch up on.

Newspapers can marry the printed word with pictures, diagrams and statistics, as can websites. But you cannot curl up on a settee with a computer! So the greatest threat to the newspaper is computer miniaturization – WAPS. Even so, these do not enable you to scan as many as 30 different stories on a spread at once, as you can with a newspaper. Papers are also far more accessible to the poor than is new technology.

More than money

The strength and future of the newspaper industry lies partly in increasing **investment**. The biggest investors are the major newspaper chains. But critics of chains claim that they are able to manipulate the public far too easily, that a whole chain can reflect the views of its proprietor or editorial director. Those in favour of chains believe that each newspaper within them has to promote a slightly different point of view or present the news in a different way, in order to remain competitive. This keeps press freedom alive.

Freedom is very important to the reader. A newspaper's 'Letters' column gives the reader their 'right to reply'. But opinion is something that the Internet allows on a much bigger scale, with interactive sites that can give participants a global view on topical issues – or a minority view if they wish. This is something that newspapers can develop on their own websites.

Annual newspaper awards reward editors, journalists and photographers for their work and help to boost sales figures. Here, editor Kenneth Best (left) accepts his 'World Press Hero' award at the International Press Institute's Awards in Boston, USA, 2000.

New attractions

Tabloid newspapers are always trying to attract a new, younger readership with giveaways, competitions and scratchcards. On the news front, they have adopted aggressive **leader** columns, dramatic headlines and '**exclusives**'. **Broadsheet** newspapers are evermore analytical, providing in-depth background, commentary and analysis on most political, financial and social issues. But they now also include lighter sections, to attract a broader audience. Local newspapers, though, are finding that they do not have to fight for popularity. They have found that there is an ever-increasing demand for real local news and information. **Desktop publishing** has enabled small groups to publish papers very cheaply. This will enable even more people to publish in the future.

Technical tips

Technical innovations will speed up the production process and therefore make news increasingly up to date. In the USA and Japan, voice recognition computers are being developed. These could end the need for reporters and **copy-takers** to key in **copy**. Ink-jet printers will in the future see an end to the age-old printing plate.

Glossary

archive a newspaper's library of past and present stories and information

artwork design features of a newspaper, such as headings, rules lines and decoration

break (the story) to publish a new story, especially an important front-page item

broadsheet large format newspaper with a lot of serious content

censor to prevent a particular story, or parts of it, from being published

communist type of government, such as that in China, based on the supposed equal distribution of wealth and property

copy written text of a news item or feature

copy editor person who makes sure that the copy is written in the correct style, without mistakes, and fits the column space (see sub-editor)

copy-taker person who receives the copy from reporters via telephone and types it into a computer

copy-taster person who accepts or rejects stories as they come into the newspaper office

democratic system of government, such as in the USA, Australia and European countries, in which the people elect their own government from a choice of political parties

desktop publishing publishing using computers and computer printers on a small scale

digital information in the form of a series of binary digits (1 and 0) that are the building blocks of computer technology

edit to select the main stories, pictures and features and to make sure that their content and written style suits the image of the paper

edition particular issue of a newspaper, for example the morning or evening edition on a certain day

Editor the person in control of the content, written style and policy of a newspaper

editorial policy establishing the kinds of story and feature that will be printed in a newspaper, its style and basic political stance

exclusive the first newspaper to publish an important story (also 'scoop' – see below)

facsimile method of electronically transmitting completed newspaper pages – the copy, pictures, advertisements and so on, so that they can be printed in a different part of the country or world

feature story or article written on a particular topic or event, such as a motor show

focus group group of people gathered together together according to their age, interests, occupations, and so on for the purposes of finding out their likes and dislikes; the results of the survey are used to focus newspaper advertising, stories, political opinion and so on

house style   written style used in a newspaper or magazine

invest   to put money into something in order to develop it and eventually get a profit from it

issue   an edition, or particular publication, of a newspaper

lay out   to fit copy and pictures on to the design of a newspaper page

leader   the most important story of the day, or of a particular section; also the editiorial comment on the main story

market research   finding out what peoples' likes and dislikes are to ensure maximum sales of a product

metros   the US term for city reporters

modem   electronic device that converts digital data (in this case pictures) into signals that can be sent to other computers via a telephone system

newsprint   cheap, coarse paper used for printing newspapers

news agency   organization that gathers news through its own reporters and networks, and then sells it to newspapers and other media

pixel   one of the thousands of tiny picture cells that make up an image on screen

press release   statement about a particular issue given out to the press by individuals, companies, organizations or governments

rights   the permission to publish information or images

romanized   put into the Roman alphabet

scoop   to uncover an important story and be the first newspaper to publish it

server   computer that stores files which can be accessed on other computers linked to it

spin-doctor   assistant to a person or organization in a powerful position – he or she makes sure that the person or organization is seen in a good light by the media

sub-editor   person who copy edits (see above) – making sure that the story is written in the correct style and fits the given space

syndicate   group of associated, or linked, newspapers, which often share information resources

tabloid   newspaper with a smaller format than the broadsheet (see above), and often containing more sensationalist stories

transparency   a colour positive photographic film; the pictures can be printed or shown as slides on a screen

typeface   particular style of type printed on the page

Index